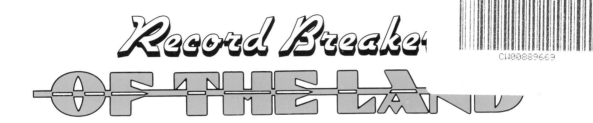

Record Breakers
OF THE LAND

Rupert Matthews

Brian Trodd Publishing House Limited

LIFE ON LAND

Biggest Flower Bloom in the World

The rafflesia plant has the biggest flower bloom in the world. The bloom is about 3 feet (90 centimetres) across and weighs as much as 22 pounds (10 kilograms).

The brownish-red flower looks like a huge cabbage and smells like rotten meat. It draws great swarms of flies, who pollinate the plants. The rafflesia smells so bad that it is also called the stinking corpse lily. It grows in the forests of Malaysia.

Heaviest Insect

The weight of a fully grown male Goliath beetle can be up to 3½ ounces (100 grams). No living insect is heavier than that.

Goliath beetles live in the African forests near the equator. They can grow to be more than 4 inches (10 centimetres) in length.

Largest Living Object

What's the largest living thing in the world? It's the "General Sherman" tree, located in Sequoia National Park, California. Sequoias are very large evergreen trees, and "General Sherman" is the largest of all. It stands 275 feet (84 metres) tall.

How tall is that? Well, if the Statue of Liberty were placed beside "General Sherman," it would be in the shade of the leaves. The Statue of Liberty is only 152 feet (46 metres) tall.

Heaviest and Tallest Dogs

The St. Bernard is one of the two heaviest breeds of dog. The other is the Old English mastiff. When fully grown, both weigh between 170 and 200 pounds (77 to 91 kilograms). The largest known of either breed is a male mastiff that weighed 314½ pounds (145 kilograms). It stood 35 inches (89 centimetres) at the shoulder.

The tallest breeds of dog are the Great Dane and the Irish wolfhound. They can both grow taller than 39 inches (99 centimetres) at the shoulder. The tallest known of either breed was a male Great Dane that died in 1984. It stood 41½ inches (105 centimetres) tall.

Simplest Animal

The animal with the simplest body is the amoeba. This tiny creature has no skeleton, no eyes, no ears, no arms, no legs, and no brain. It is hardly more than a blob of living jelly. A simple nucleus controls the amoeba's movements. It reproduces itself by just splitting in two.

There are many different amoebas, and they live in many different places. Some live inside other animals, *including* people.

5

Fastest Mammals on Land

Over a short distance, no land animal moves faster than the cheetah. This spotted cat hunts gazelles and antelopes on the open plains of Africa and Asia. The cheetah sneaks up as close as it can to its prey, then suddenly dashes forward. In two seconds the cheetah will be running at a speed of 45 miles (72 kilometres) per hour. After that, it quickly reaches a peak speed of about 63 miles (100 kilometres) per hour.

With luck, the cheetah catches its prey. It not, it gives up the chase.

Over a long distance, no land animal moves faster than the pronghorn antelope. It lives on the western plains of North America. A pronghorn antelope can average 43 miles (69 kilometres) per hour over about 6 miles (10 kilometres).

Greatest Animal Leaper

Kangaroos are great leapers and jumpers that live in Australia and New Guinea. The largest is the red kangaroo. It's about 7 feet (2 metres) tall and weighs as much as 175 pounds (79 kilograms). Each of its leaps is about 20 feet (6 metres) long. In January 1951, a red kangaroo leaped 42 feet (13 metres). That is still the longest ever recorded.

How high can a red kangaroo jump? A boomer, or large male, was once seen clearing a 10-foot (3-metre) fence very easily.

Fastest Running Bird

The ostrich is a true record breaker. It cannot fly, but it is the fastest-running, heaviest and tallest of all birds. And it lays the largest egg.

The ostrich can run at a steady speed of 30 miles (50 kilometres) per hour. Its top speed is about 44 miles (70 kilometres) per hour.

The ostrich lives in the open plains and dry grasslands of Africa. The adult male weighs about 300 pounds (136 kilograms) and is about 8 feet (2½ metres) tall. A few ostriches are even larger.

Smallest Farmers

In the forests of South America live the parasol ants, the world's smallest farmers. These ants get their name from the way they carry pieces of leaf over their heads. They look as if they're carrying parasols, or small umbrellas.

Just ½ inch (1 centimetre) long, parasol ants are also called leaf-cutter ants. It's easy to see why. Worker ants cut small bits of leaf from the jungle plants. Then they carry the leaf bits into their nests underground. There, worker ants chew up the leaf bits and lay the chewed bits, or pulp, in long rows. After that, they plant spores, or tiny seeds, of a fungus on the pulp. The fungus is like bread mould. When the mould has grown, the worker ants harvest it to feed the thousands of ants in the colony.

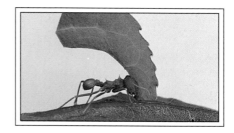

Biggest Cat

A Siberian tiger almost 11 feet (3½ metres) long and weighing over 900 pounds (410 kilograms) is the largest cat alive. It lives on an animal preserve in New Jersey. The average Siberian tiger is more than 10 feet (3 metres) long and 3½ feet (1 metre) tall. Its weight is about 585 pounds (265 kilograms).

Tigers are the most powerful members of the cat family. They kill smaller creatures such as deer with a single swipe of a claw and larger animals by biting the neck.

Slowest Mammal

The rain forests of South America hide many odd animals. One of them is the three-toed sloth. It is the slowest mammal in the world. This creature feeds at night on leaves and fruits. And it goes after fresh food very, very slowly.

Noisiest Snakes

Most snakes are silent animals. Rattlesnakes are different. They deliberately make rattling noises to frighten away large animals that might not know the snake is there.

The snake's rattles are hollow segments of hard, dead skin. When shaken, the rattles bump against one another and make a noise. The rattles often break off. But the snake sheds its skin three times a year. Each time it does, the snake gets another rattle.

The average speed of the three-toed sloth on the ground is about 7 feet (2 metres) per minute. In the trees, it is faster, moving up to 15 feet (4½ metres) per minute. A sloth was once seen to move 8 feet (about 2½ metres) in 30 seconds. This is the speed record for sloths!

Largest Living Land Animal

The African bush elephant is the largest land animal alive today. It can grow as tall as 12 feet (3 metres) at the shoulder and weigh more than 6 tons.

Home for the African bush elephants is in the forests and grasslands of central Africa. Usually, they travel in herds. They are almost always on the move, looking for fresh plants to eat.

Most Fearless Hunter

Unlike most meat-eaters, a wolverine *will* attack an animal larger or stronger than itself. What it lacks in size, the wolverine more than makes up for in fierceness. It is almost never afraid.

The wolverine lives in northern and western parts of North America as well as in Europe and Asia. When a wolverine is fully grown, it weighs between 35 and 60 pounds (16 to 27 kilograms). Its length is 3 to 3½ feet (90 to 105 centimetres). That includes an 8-inch (20-centimetre) tail.

Usually, the wolverine will hunt small creatures such as hares and lemmings. But it has been known to attack and kill a bull moose. And it can drive off bears and wolves that come too close.

Largest Beaver Dam

No animal can match the building skills of the American beaver. It builds a dam and a lodge of branches and mud.

The largest beaver dam known was found on the Jefferson River in Montana in the 1970s. It is 2,296 feet (700 metres) long.

Tallest Living Animal

The giraffe is the tallest land animal alive. It roams the dry scrub land of Africa. The male giraffe can reach a height of about 18 feet (5½ metres) to the top of his head and about 11 feet (about 3 metres) to his shoulder. Females are about 3 feet (90 centimetres) shorter.

With its long neck, the giraffe is able to browse on treetop leaves.

Largest Land Animal of All Time

Was it a dinosaur? The answer is yes. The biggest known dinosaur is called Seismosaurus (SIZE-moe-SORE-us). Its name means "earthquake lizard." When this huge plant-eater moved around, the ground probably rumbled like an earthquake was passing by!

The bones of Seismosaurus were found in New Mexico in 1988. Seismosaurus was between 100 and 120 feet (30 to 40 metres) long. It weighed about 89 tons (90 metric tons). And it lived about 130 million years ago in North America.

Largest Ape

In the movies, King Kong was a giant gorilla that climbed the Empire State Building. No apes are ever that large. But the largest and the strongest apes *are* the gorillas.

When they stand on their hind legs, the largest male gorillas are 6 feet (nearly 2 metres) tall.

In the wild, males weigh up to 450 pounds (210 kilograms). In zoos they sometimes get fat and can weigh as much as 600 pounds (275 kilograms).

Gorillas look fierce and are strong, but in fact they are peaceful plant-eaters.

TRANSPORTATION

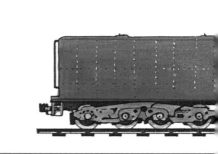

Champion Locomotive

The 2900 Class 4-8-4s were the heaviest and longest steam passenger locomotives ever made. They each weighed 961,000 pounds (436,818 kilograms) and were 121 feet (37 metres) long. They began in 1944, and ran between Kansas City and Los Angeles. They regularly travelled 1,760 miles (2,830 kilometres) without needing to change the locomotive, and this is another record. Number 2903 is on exhibition at the Museum of Science and Industry, Chicago.

Longest Bicycle in the World

A bicycle built for 35? That's how many riders the world's longest bicycle can carry. Made in Belgium in 1979, it is nearly 67 feet (20 metres) long.

Train-Ship Collision

One dark night in February 1913, a strange collision took place in the town of Cumberland, Mississippi. A flood had covered the railway tracks there several feet deep. The *Lochie S*, a small passenger boat that sat very high in the water, was steaming along the flooded tracks. That's when a freight train came down the tracks and crashed into the boat. Luckily, no one was hurt.

First American Transcontinental Railroad

The first rail line to cross the American West was completed on 10 May 1869. On that day, the Central Pacific and the Union Pacific joined tracks at Promontory, Utah, north of Great Salt Lake. The tracks the two companies built ran from Omaha, Nebraska, to Sacramento, California and were connected to rail lines on the East Coast.

Later that year, the railway from Sacramento to Oakland, across the bay from San Francisco, was opened.

Finally, in 1877, a bridge was completed across the Missouri River near Omaha.

World's Longest Limousine

You would be riding in elegance in "the American Dream." That's the name of the world's longest limousine. It is 60 feet (18 metres) long and weighs 20,000 pounds (9,100 kilograms). This Cadillac car has 16 wheels and 2 engines, one in the front and one in the rear. It takes 2 people to drive it. The drivers wear headphones and talk to each other by radio.

Fastest Elevators With Passengers

There is a diamond mine shaft that goes down 6,800 feet (2,072 metres) in the Western Deep mine in Transvaal. The elevator cage there can travel at a speed of 41 miles (66 kilometres) per hour.

That is almost twice the speed of the fastest public elevators. These are in the Sunshine 60 building in Tokyo, Japan. They go up to the top floor, the sixtieth, at a speed of nearly 23 miles (37 kilometres) per hour.

Longest Road

The Pan-American Highway is the longest road in the world. It runs from northwest Alaska to Santiago, Chile. (There is a gap of 250 miles, or 400 kilometres, in Panama and Colombia.) From Santiago, the highway goes eastward to Buenos Aires in Argentina. Then it turns north to rasilia in Brazil. The Pan-American Highway is more than 15,000 miles (24,000 kilometres) long.

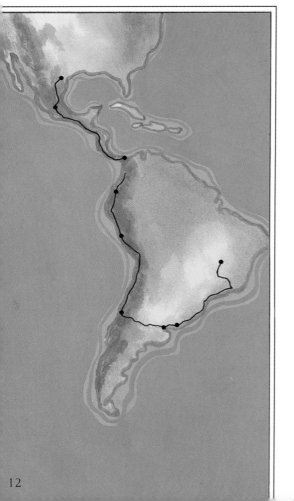

Fastest Bicycle Trip Across America

In July 1986, the fastest times by bicycle across the United States were set in the McDonald's Race Across America. The race started in Huntington Beach, California. It finished in Atlantic City, New Jersey. The distance was 3,107 miles (5,000 kilometres).

Pete Penseyres was the winning male cyclist. He crossed the country in 8 days 9 hours 47 minutes. The fastest woman was Elaine Mariolle. Her time was 10 days 2 hours 4 minutes.

World's Top High-Altitude Canoeists

Mount Everest is the highest mountain in the world. In September 1976, Dr. Michael Jones and Michael Hopkinson decided to *canoe* down it. Both were members of the British Everest Canoe Expedition.

They began their ride 17,500 feet (5,334 metres) above sea level – at the source of the River Dudh Kosi in Nepal. And the two canoeists made it. What a ride!

Single-Span Bridge

The Humber Estuary Bridge in Britain has the longest single span, or distance between two supports in the world. It stretches for 1,542 yards (1,410 metres). The bridge's total length is 2,428 yards (2,220 metres).

Most Successful Monorail

The word *monorail* means "one rail." The most successful monorail yet made is in Wuppertal, West Germany. This rail line is 8 miles (13 kilometres) long. It has been running since 1901. By 1960, it had carried about one *billion* passengers.

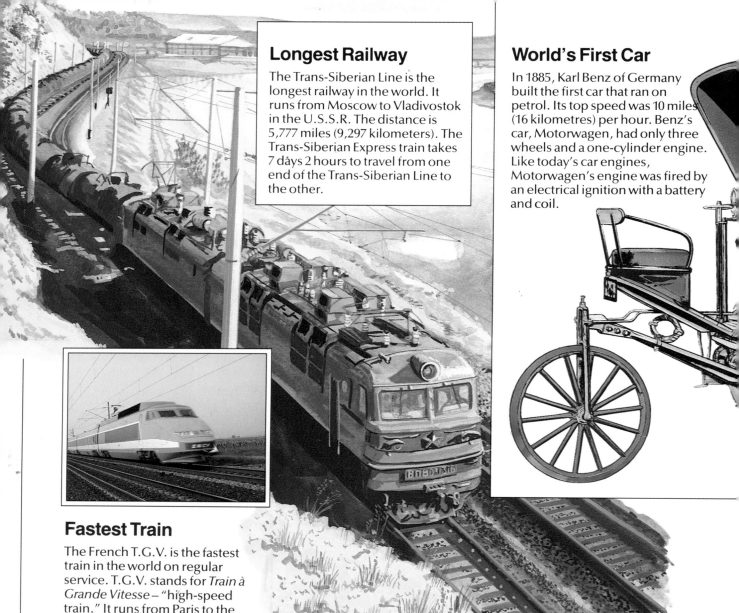

Longest Railway

The Trans-Siberian Line is the longest railway in the world. It runs from Moscow to Vladivostok in the U.S.S.R. The distance is 5,777 miles (9,297 kilometers). The Trans-Siberian Express train takes 7 days 2 hours to travel from one end of the Trans-Siberian Line to the other.

World's First Car

In 1885, Karl Benz of Germany built the first car that ran on petrol. Its top speed was 10 miles (16 kilometres) per hour. Benz's car, Motorwagen, had only three wheels and a one-cylinder engine. Like today's car engines, Motorwagen's engine was fired by an electrical ignition with a battery and coil.

Fastest Train

The French T.G.V. is the fastest train in the world on regular service. T.G.V. stands for *Train à Grande Vitesse* – "high-speed train." It runs from Paris to the Mediterranean. The T.G.V. averages 132 miles (212 kilometres) per hour from Paris to Lyon, its first stop. Sometimes it reaches 170 miles (273 kilometres) per hour.

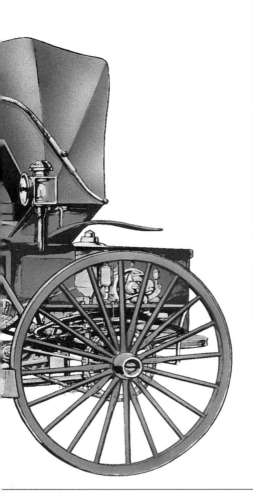

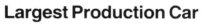

Land Speed Record

Can you imagine going more than 600 miles per hour in a car? Richard Noble of Great Britain can. He did it on 4 October 1983. The jet-powered car he was driving, *Thrust 2*, reached a speed of 633 miles (1,019 kilometres) per hour. He zoomed across Black Rock Desert in Nevada, setting a new one-mile land speed record.

Actually, Richard Noble raced twice. The two runs he made were in opposite directions. That way, the speed of the car couldn't be helped by a strong wind or ground slope in just one direction. So Noble's speed was an average of his two runs that day.

Nearly four years earlier, in December 1979, Stan Barrett of the United States drove a car faster than Noble did. Barrett drove a rocket-powered car called the *Budweiser Rocket* 739 miles (1,190 kilometres) per hour at Edwards Air Force Base in California. But he made only a single run. So his speed is not in the official record books.

Largest Production Car

The Bugatti "Royale" Type 41 was the largest car ever to be put into production. Beginning in 1927, six of these cars were manufactured in France by Ettore Bugatti of Italy. The car had an 8-cylinder engine and was more than 22 feet (about 7 metres) long. Larger cars have been built, but they were custom-made and one of a kind.

SPORTS

Greatest Golfers of All Time

The world's major golf tournaments are the PGA, British Open, U.S. Open, Masters, and U.S. Amateur championships. Only one golfer has ever won all five of these tournaments twice – Jack Nicklaus. He has won a record 20 major tournaments in his career. Overall, Nicklaus has 71 PGA tournament wins to his credit. This last total is second only to Sam Snead's 84 victories.

In 1930, Bobby Jones won the U.S. Open, the British Open, the U.S. Amateur, and the British Amateur golf titles. No other golfer has ever done that in the same year. Among Jones's many victories were 4 U.S. Open and 5 U.S. Amateur championships. He and Nicklaus are often mentioned at the best golfers in history.

Highest Paid Woman Athlete

American tennis player Martina Navratilova is the highest paid woman athlete of all time. By the end of 1988, she had earned more than £8,000,000. This *doesn't* include money from advertising and sponsorships.

In 1984, she won 74 straight singles matches, a modern record. By 1989, she had 17 Grand Slam singles titles. This is not the record. Margaret Court of Australia won 24 Grand Slam singles titles.

Best Test Cricketers

The following cricketers have made more runs or taken more wickets than anybody else in international cricket matches.

Sunil Gavaskar (India) has made 10,122 runs in 125 test matches. He is followed by Allan Border (Australia) with 8,273 runs from 108 test matches and Geoffrey Boycott (England) with 8,114 runs also from 108 test matches.

Richard Hadlee (New Zealand) is the world's greatest wicket-taker: 396 in 79 test matches. Next is Ian Botham (England) with 376 from 97 tests followed by Dennis Lillee (Australia) with 355 from 70 tests.

Most Successful Grand Prix Driver

The driver with the most points in World Championship Grand Prix motor racing is Alain Prost of France. He has over 500 Grand Prix points, and has won 39 races. Prost was also world champion in 1985 and in 1986.

Greatest Hitting Streak of All Time

In 1941, New York Yankee center fielder Joe DiMaggio hit safely in 56 straight games. That broke the major-league baseball hitting streak record set by Willie Keeler in 1897.

DiMaggio started his hitting streak against the Chicago White Sox on 15 May 1941. He got a single. The streak ended in mid-July against the Cleveland Indians. During that 56-game period, DiMaggio collected 91 hits in 223 at-bats. He finished the season batting .357 .

Youngest Men's Wimbledon Champion

Boris Becker of West Germany won his first Grand Slam tennis title at Wimbledon in 1985. He is the youngest male Wimbledon champion ever. Becker's age then was 17 years 7 months. He won Wimbledon again in 1986 and 1989.

Biggest Attendance at a Soccer Match

On 16 July 1950 a crowd of 203,500 were packed into the Maracana Stadium, Rio de Janeiro in Brazil. They were watching the final match of the World Cup, between Brazil and Uruguay. Uruguay won the match 2-1.

Longest Ski Jump

Poland's Piotr Fijas made the longest ski jump on record. He jumped 636 feet (194 metres) at Planica, Yugoslavia, on 14 March 1987.

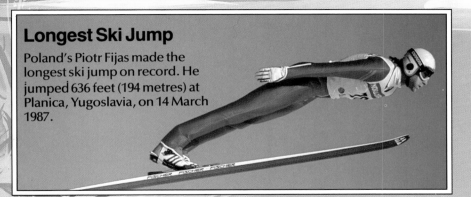

Longest Le Mans Auto Race

The 24-hour race held every year at Le Mans, France, tests the endurance of both drivers and machines. The winner is the car, with its team of three drivers, that travels the greatest distance in 24 hours.

The greatest distance so far was in the 1988 race. A British team driving a Jaguar went 3,313 miles (5,332 kilometres). Their speed over the Le Mans course was 138 miles (222 kilometres) per hour.

Fastest Human

This unofficial title goes to the sprinter who has the fastest official time in the 100-metre race. U.S. racer Carl Lewis (above right) is thus the world's fastest human. He set the official record on 24 September 1988, at the Olympics in Seoul, South Korea. Lewis ran the 100-metre final race in 9.92 seconds. Canadian sprinter Ben Johnson ran the same race in 9.79 seconds. But he was later stripped of his gold medal and world record because of drug use.

The fastest woman alive is Florence Griffith-Joyner ("Flo-Jo") of the United States. On 16 July 1988, she ran a 100-metre race in 10.49 seconds. Later that year, she won the Olympic gold medal.

Longest Jump

Bob Beamon of the United States set the world long-jump record in 1968. He won the gold medal at the Olympics in Mexico City with a jump of 29 feet 2½ inches (nearly 9 metres). That broke the previous world record by an astonishing 1 foot 9 inches (53 centimetres).

Most Capped Soccer Players

Pat Jennings, the former Northern Ireland goalkeeper, made 119 appearances for his country between 1964 and 1986. The next three most capped players are Bjorn Nordqvist (Sweden) with 115; Dino Zoff (Italy) with 112 and Pele (Brazil) with 110. Dino Zoff was also captain of the Italian team that won the World Cup in 1982. Pele played for Brazil when they won the World Cup in 1958, 1962 and 1970.

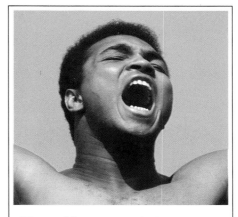

Best Heavyweights

Joe Louis (born in 1914) was heavyweight champion for longer than any other boxer. He won the title in 1937 by knocking out James J. Braddock. He defended it a record 25 times before he retired undefeated in 1949. Louis later returned to the ring but could not regain his title.

Muhammad Ali (born in 1942) regained his heavyweight title twice. He first became champion in 1964 when he knocked out Sonny Liston. Ali won it a second time in 1974 by knocking out George Foreman. Through ten bouts over the next four years, Muhammad Ali held on to his title. He was finally beaten by Leon Spinks in February 1978. Ali, however, fought Spinks in a return match seven months later and took the title back. Muhammad Ali retired in 1979.

Rocky Marciano (born in 1923) is the only world heavyweight champion who never lost a professional fight. He fought 49 bouts and won them all.

First Four-Minute Mile

Until the year 1954, no one in the world had run a mile (1.61 kilometres) in less than four minutes. Some experts said that no one could ever run that fast. But an English medical student named Roger Bannister proved them wrong.

On 6 May 1954, he ran at a meeting in Oxford, England, and thousands came to watch. Bannister ran a fast race, and people could see he had come very close to breaking the four-minute barrier. They waited to hear the official time. The announcer got as far as the word "three" when the crowd's cheers drowned out the rest. Bannister had run the mile in 3 minutes 59.4 seconds.

Many athletes have run a faster mile since 1954. The current record of 3 minutes 46.32 seconds was set in 1985 by Steve Cram of Great Britain. But no race has been more dramatic than Bannister's run.

Champion Bronco

A bronco is a wild or half-wild horse. That's why horses used in bronco-riding contests buck and gallop so fiercely. They're not used to riders on their backs.

One bronco in particular took a strong dislike to riders. That was a Canadian horse named Midnight. At the annual Calgary Stampede in Alberta, Canada, Midnight shook off riders at will. In 12 years, no Calgary Stampede rider was ever able to stay atop Midnight for longer than 2 or 3 seconds.

Most Runners in a Marathon

Run over a distance of 26 miles 385 yards (about 42 kilometres), the marathon has become very popular. The ninth London Marathon, held in April 1989, had the most runners so far. An estimated 27,000 took part, and 22,587 finished the course. Both figures are records. Who won? Kenya's Douglas Wakiihuri crossed the finish line first for the men. Britain's Veronique Marot did likewise for the women.

Fastest Speed in the Indianapolis 500

The Indianapolis 500 race in America was first run in 1911. It covers 500 miles (800 kilometres) over 200 laps of the track. The greatest lap speed ever reached was 221 miles (356 kilometres) per hour by Mario Andretti of the United States in 1988.

The fastest Indianapolis 500 race (2 hours 55 minutes 42.48 seconds) was won by Bobby Rahal of the United States in 1986.

Greatest Scorer in a Pro Basketball Game

On 2 March 1962, Wilt Chamberlain of the Philadelphia Warriors scored 100 points in a game against the New York Knicks. The Warrior center hit 36 of 63 field-goal tries and 28 of 32 free throws. At the time, Chamberlain's total was 29 points more than the previous single-game scoring record. The final score that 2 March was 169–147 in favour of Philadelphia.

Most Points in a Pro Football Career

Only one man has scored more than 2,000 points playing football over his entire professional career. He is George Blanda, who played for the Chicago Bears, Baltimore Colts, Houston Oilers, and Oakland Raiders between 1949 and 1975. All in all, Blanda scored 2,002 points: 9 touchdowns, 943 points after touchdown, and 335 field goals. He also holds the record for the most seasons played (26) and the most games in his career (340).

GEOGRAPHY

Snowiest Place

Imagine living in a place where in one year more than a hundred feet of snow can fall! That place is Mount Rainier National Park in the state of Washington. Between February 1971 and February 1972, 102 feet (31 metres) of snow fell in the Paradise area of the park. That's about 1,225 inches of snow. Each winter, the resort hotel there props up its walls with beams on the inside. Why? So the building won't fall in under the snow's weight!

Largest Desert

The Sahara is the world's largest desert. It's in northern Africa and covers 3,250,000 square miles (8,400,000 square kilometres). This makes the Sahara larger than all of western Europe.

At its widest point, the Sahara stretches for 3,200 miles (5,150 kilometres) from east to west. From north to south, it measures as much as 1,400 miles (2,250 kilometres).

World's Largest National Park

Canada has the largest national park in the world. Wood Buffalo National Park covers 17,560 square miles (45,480 square kilometres). In acres, that comes out as well over eleven *million*. The park is in the northern part of the province of Alberta, Canada. It is so large that a country such as Switzerland could easily fit inside Wood Buffalo National Park.

Longest River

Most people say that the Nile is the world's longest river, but not everyone agrees. It depends on what you decide is a part of a river.

The Nile River's length from its source above Lake Victoria to the Mediterranean Sea is 4,145 miles (6,670 kilometres).

The Amazon River is 4,000 miles (6,437 kilometres) long. That is measured from its source high in the Andes Mountains down its main channel to the sea. But there is a branch of the Amazon that follows a more winding course. This is 4,195 miles (6,750 kilometres) long. So there are some who say the Amazon is longer than the Nile.

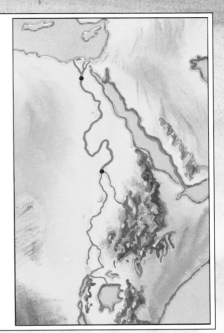

Strongest Earthquake

On 22 May 1960, the strongest earthquake ever recorded took place in Lebu, Chile. The Kanamori Scale for measuring earthquakes ranges from "1", the weakest, to "10," the strongest. On that scale, the 1960 Chilean earthquake registered 9.5. Five thousand people were killed.

The most famous earthquake in the United States occurred in San Francisco on 18 April 1906. It was nearly as strong as the Chilean earthquake. In some places the ground moved sideways as much as 21 feet (about 6½ metres). More than 650 people died or disappeared. And some 28,000 buildings were destroyed.

Longest Natural Arch

Landscape Arch in the Arches National Park near Moab, Utah, is the world's longest known arch. It is 291 feet (88 metres) long. The Arches National Park is small (115 square miles). Still, more natural arches can be seen in that small area in one day than anywhere else in the world.

How does a natural arch form? Wind, rain, and frost wear away at sandstone over hundreds of years. Sometimes, this erosion will force big, gaping holes in huge blocks of sandstone. That can leave long, thick ridges. Erosion continues, narrowing these ridges into long, natural arches.

Oldest Rocks on Earth

The earth was formed about 4,500 million years ago, but no rocks from that long ago have every been found. The oldest rocks ever found, zircon crystals, lie in Western Australia. They are about 4,300 million years old.

There is a chunk of gneiss (pronounced "nice") from Greenland dated at 3,750 million years. And a piece of granite was found in Minnesota that is between 3,700 and 3,900 million years old.

Chain of Volcanoes

The longest volcanic chain in the world is the "Ring of Fire", which encircles the Pacific Ocean. From Tierra del Fuego in South America, the volcanoes run north along the Andes to North America. Mount St. Helens which erupted on 18 May 1980 is a part of it. The chain runs on through Siberia and the eastern U.S.S.R. to Japan, the Philippines, and New Zealand. It is approximately 27,000 miles (41,600 kilometres) long.

Lowest Land and Saltiest Inland Sea

Nowhere on earth is dry land farther below sea level than on the shores of the Dead Sea, which borders Israel and Jordan. The land around the Dead Sea lies 1,300 feet (396 metres) below sea level.

Streams carrying mineral salts from nearby hills flow into the Dead Sea. No water flows out of it. The Dead Sea is eight times as salty as the oceans of the world.

Greatest Monoliths

A monolith is a single block of stone. Mount Augustus in the desert of Western Australia is the largest known monolith. It is 1,237 feet (377 metres) high and 5 miles (8 kilometres) long. Ayers Rock in the Northern Territory of Australia (illustrated) is much better known, but not as large. It is more than 1,100 feet (340 metres) high. A path around it is more than 5 miles (8 kilometres) long.

Highest Mountains

Mount Everest lies in the Great Himalayan range that rises in Nepal and Tibet. Its summit is 29,028 feet (8,848 metres) above sea level.

Mauna Kea, a volcanic mountain in Hawaii, is much higher than Mount Everest. But its base is at the bottom of the Pacific Ocean. Mauna Kea measures 33,476 feet (10,203 metres) high, but only 13,796 feet (4,204 metres) is above sea level.

Highest Waterfall

Looking for gold in Venezuela, American pilot Jimmy Angel saw something else in 1935. Below the plane he was flying over a branch of the Carrao River was the highest waterfall in the world. It is 3,212 feet (980 metres) from top to bottom. The longest single descent the water makes is 2,648 feet (808 metres).

Angel was not the first person to discover this waterfall. Indians of the region knew about it for many years. And a Spanish explorer named Ernesto Sanchez La Cruz also reported it in 1910. But the waterfall was named after Jimmy Angel – *Salto Angel*. It means "Angel Falls".

Greatest Crater Lake

The largest lake inside the crater of a volcano is Crater Lake in the Cascade Mountains of Oregon. The eruption that made the crater took place about 7,000 years ago. It blew a hole in the earth that is 6 miles (10 kilometres) across and up to 4,000 feet (1,200 metres) deep. This great hole slowly began to fill with water that fell as rain and snow, and the lake now is nearly 2,000 feet (608 metres) deep.

Largest Cave

In 1980, a huge cavern was discovered in Sarawak, Borneo. It is 2,300 feet (700 metres) long, 980 feet (300 metres) wide, and at least 230 feet (70 metres) high. The longest system of connected caves lies beneath Mammoth Cave National Park in Kentucky. There are more than 300 miles (483 kilometres) of passages.

Largest Freshwater Lakes

Lake Superior, the largest of the Great Lakes, covers more surface than any other freshwater lake. It has an area of 31,800 square miles (82,300 square kilometres).

Lake Baikal in southern Siberia, however, has more water than any other freshwater lake. It is the world's deepest lake, more than a mile deep in places. It holds an enormous volume of water. There are about 5,600 cubic miles (23,000 cubic kilometres) of fresh water in Lake Baikal. That's about the same amount of water in all five Great Lakes combined.

Largest Canyon

The Grand Canyon is not called "grand" for nothing. Located in Arizona, it is the largest canyon in the world. This great gorge cut by the Colorado River is 217 miles (349 kilometres) long and from 4 to 18 miles (6½ to 30 kilometres) wide. At its deepest, the Grand Canyon measures more than a mile (1,600 metres) from rim to river. The flow of the Colorado River through the canyon is slower since the Glen Canyon Dam to the north was built in 1964. But the river's work of erosion in the Grand Canyon goes on, deepening it.

Greatest Explosion

The world's greatest explosion blew apart the island of Krakatoa on 27 August 1883. When the volcano beneath the island erupted, more than 4 cubic miles (18 cubic kilometres) of rock were blown to pieces. These pieces were thrown up in a huge column as much as 33 miles (53 kilometres) high. A huge tidal wave more than 100 feet (30 metres) high swept past Java and Sumatra. It killed more than 36,000 people, and reached as far as Cape Horn, at the tip of South America, before it died away.

Sounds of the blast were heard, as loud as thunder, 3,000 miles (4,800 kilometres) away.

World's Most Extreme Climate

The widest range of temperature in one place is in Verkhoyansk, Siberia. There, the winter temperature can drop to 90° below zero Fahrenheit (−68° Celsius). The blazing July sun can send the temperature up to 98° Fahrenheit (36° Celsius).

Coldest Place on Earth

The lowest temperature ever recorded was −128.6° Fahrenheit (−89.2° Celsius) taken in Antarctica in 1983. In Northern America, the coldest winter on record was the winter of 1988-89. Towns in the interior of Alaska had temperatures down to −75° Fahrenheit (−59.4° Celsius) for days at a time.

FASCINATING FACTS

Outstanding Nobel Prize Winners

Marie Curie was the first woman to win a Nobel Prize. She was also the first woman to win a Nobel Prize twice. In 1903, she shared the Nobel Prize for Physics with her husband, Pierre Curie, as well as Henri Becquerel. They discovered radioactivity. In 1911, Marie Curie was given the Nobel Prize for Chemistry for the discovery of radium. This time, the prize was given to her alone.

Linus Pauling of the United States is the only person who has won both a scientific and non-scientific Nobel Prize. He was awarded the Nobel Prize for Chemistry in 1954 and the Nobel Peace Prize in 1962.

Hardest Substance

A diamond is the hardest substance that occurs naturally in the world. It is five times harder than the second-hardest substance, corundum.

Of the many different kinds of diamonds, probably the hardest is the rare black diamond of Borneo. It is too hard to be polished by industrial diamonds, which is the way most diamonds get their gleam. A Borneo black diamond can only be polished with the dust from other Borneo black diamonds.

First Woman on a Police Force

Alice Wells became the first policewoman in history when she joined the Los Angeles Police Department in September 1910.

Oldest Statue

The Great Sphinx near Cairo, Egypt, is the oldest large statue in the world. No one knows exactly how old it is, but it is older than the Great Pyramid near it. That was built in about 2800 B.C.

The Great Sphinx was carved

out of a hill of solid sandstone by men who had no modern tools. It has the body of a lion and a human head. Some say the head is a portrait of Khafre, an early pharoah (king) of Egypt. The statue is 66 feet (20 metres) above the desert floor and it is 240 feet (73 metres) long.

Deepest and Hottest Mines

The record is held by a gold mine in South Africa that goes down to a depth of 12,390 feet (3,777 metres). The men working in this gold mine are more than 2 miles (3½ kilometres) beneath the surface of the earth.

Before that gold mine was made, the deepest mine on earth was a coal mine in West Virginia. It is 7,500 feet (2,250 metres) deep. This mine still holds another record. The heat of the rock walls at the bottom is a constant 168° Fahrenheit (74° Celsius). That is much hotter than the gold mine.

Strangest Near-Accident at Work

In 1937, a farm worker was ploughing a wheat field near Potwin, Kansas. As the man was driving his tractor across the field, he saw the land crack open. In seconds, a huge section of the field vanished. Some 22,500 square feet (2,090 square metres) just disappeared in a cloud of dust and water spray. The man barely managed to stop his tractor at the edge of the great hole. Below the field had been an undiscovered cave with an underground stream running through it. Without any warning, the cave had fallen in.

Longest Place Name in Use

The place name still in use that has the most letters is quite a mouthful! It's Taumatawhakatang-ihangakoauauotamateaturipukak-apikimaungahoronukupokaiwhe-nuakitanatahu. This place name has 85 letters. It is the name the Maoris gave a hill on North Island, New Zealand. The Maoris are the native people of this island. The island's name means "the summit where Tamatea, who travelled all over the country, played his flute to his loved one."

Fastest Tiddlywinker

Tiddlywinks is a game where players snap small plastic disks into a cup or pot by pressing their edges with a larger disk. Players must each pot 24 winks, or disks, from a distance of at least 18 inches (45 centimetres) from the pot. The player with the fastest time wins. In 1966, Stephen Williams potted his 24 winks in just 22 seconds. That is still the world record.

Longest Motorcycle Jump

Even the great daredevil Evel Knievel never jumped as far on a motorcycle as Todd Seeley did. On 28 February 1988, Seeley rode a motorcycle 246 feet (75 metres) through the air in Tampa, Florida. It was the longest ramp-to-ramp motorcyle jump ever made.

Multiplying Mice

How many mice do you think have been born in a single litter? The record is a staggering 34 to a pet house mouse from Blackpool, England in 1982. Normally there are about 10 baby mice in a litter.

Most Telephones

Only one country in the world has more telephones than people – Monaco. For every 1,000 people there are 1,071 telephones.

Top Domino Toppling

The most dominoes anyone has ever set up at one time is 1½ million. This was done by 30 students from 3 universities in Holland. On 2 January 1988, one push toppled 1,382,101 of the dominoes. They took almost an hour to fall.

Most Television Sets

The tiny Pacific island of Guam has 700 TV sets for every 1,000 people. This is the highest concentration of TV sets in the world.

Ski Trip to South Pole

In January 1989, Shirley Metz and Victoria Murden of the United States became the first women in the world to reach the South Pole under their own power. Their ski trip took 51 days.

Biggest Hog

"Big Bill," a hog that lived on a farm near Jackson, Tennessee, was the world's heaviest ever. When it died in 1933, this Poland-China hog weighed 2,552 pounds or 1,157 kilograms. This is more than a ton!